Oxford basics
for children

LISTEN AND DO

See the Oxford University Press ELT website at ⁄
http://www.oup.com/elt for further details.

Oxford basics for children

Listen and Do

HANA ŠVECOVÁ

OXFORD
UNIVERSITY PRESS

OXFORD
UNIVERSITY PRESS

Great Clarendon Street, Oxford OX2 6DP

Oxford University Press is a department of the University of Oxford.
It furthers the University's objective of excellence in research, scholarship,
and education by publishing worldwide in

Oxford New York

Auckland Cape Town Dar es Salaam Hong Kong Karachi
Kuala Lumpur Madrid Melbourne Mexico City Nairobi
New Delhi Shanghai Taipei Toronto

With offices in

Argentina Austria Brazil Chile Czech Republic France Greece
Guatemala Hungary Italy Japan South Korea Poland Portugal
Singapore Switzerland Thailand Turkey Ukraine Vietnam

OXFORD and OXFORD ENGLISH are registered trade marks of
Oxford University Press in the UK and in certain other countries

ISBN: 978 0 19 442240 6

Printed in China

Contents

Introduction

Introduction

Listen and Do is a collection of thirty classroom activities for children aged 4–12. The activities help learners understand language by listening to instructions and performing them. Movement and physical involvement are natural and non-threatening ways for children to learn. By listening to instructions and following them, children can develop understanding before they speak. Physical response not only activates their memory and teaches them to think in the language, but it also makes learning enjoyable, playful, and fun.

Who is the book for?

The book is a useful resource for teachers of young and very young children. It provides teaching ideas and materials for a range of 'listen and do' activities. The teachers can use them:

- as a supplementary material to their course
- as fun activities that enable learners to move and integrate movement into learning
- as ice-breakers and low-anxiety activities to help learners become more confident in their contact with English
- to introduce new topics in class
- to practise listening skills and comprehension.

How the units are organized

Each unit starts with a short introduction to help you plan the activity. The introduction contains the following headings:

- **Target language:** tells you what vocabulary or language is introduced or practised in the activity.
- **Resources:** lists all the resources and props you need to do the activity in class.
- **Preparation:** explains what you should do and prepare before the lesson.
- **Time guide:** suggests how much time you need for the activity. The activities have different time requirements. There are some that only ask for five or ten minutes, others need thirty minutes or more. The time guide may help you plan in which part of your lesson you could do the activity and how it may fit in your overall lesson plan.
- **Age group:** informs you which age group the activity is suitable for. The activities have been designed to suit very young and young learners aged 4–12. Some of them work better with the learners at the younger end, who are just beginning to absorb words and phrases in English and who do that by playing and doing simple activities. Some are more suitable for the slightly older end of

learners, who are more experienced, have used the four skills (speaking, listening, reading, and writing) and are able to deal with more complex language. Many activities that suit very young children can be adapted for older learners.

Comprehension

Since meaning is taught through actions in the activities, it is important that the teacher uses a lot of body language in class. You can point at objects, show what you mean, mime, make gestures or facial expressions, and let the learners imitate the actions. It will help them understand the meaning and remember it. Similarly, you can also check understanding through actions. Let the learners follow the instructions and perform. In this way, you can see if they understand.

Encouragement and motivation

Praise children for everything they have achieved and learnt. A feeling of success and achievement motivates children and makes them feel good. Learning is more effective when children feel confident and secure, when you manage to involve them using positive feedback – 'Well done!' 'Excellent!' 'Very good!' Also, mistakes can be corrected in a friendly manner. Let children try again, encourage them to continue until they get it – 'Try again!' 'That's better.' 'That's almost right.'

Games and competition

Most activities in the book can be played as games. Every game should have a winner, but it is also important to involve the players that are out of the game. For example, in *Have a ball!*, children stand in a circle and play. All the players that make a mistake are out and have to leave the original circle. But you can ask them to start a new circle and continue playing there. In this way, they are still involved and active. Or, in *Flowers*, the learners sing and move around a circle of chairs. In each round one player who fails to find a free chair to sit on is out. There are always ways to find an additional activity for these children. For example, they can help you move the chairs and continue singing outside the circle.

Classroom layout

In some activities learners have to move around to perform the task and they need some space. If the desks and seats in your classroom are not built-in or fixed, you can push them up against the walls and use the free space in the centre for the activity. You may use the chairs to form a circle in the middle or sit on the ground on mats or cushions. If you cannot change the arrangement, try to make the best of the space available, i.e. the aisles between the rows of desks, the space in front of the board or at the back. You can divide the learners into groups and let each of them use one of the spaces. Always make sure that the learners have enough space not to bump into each other or hurt themselves.

Inside versus outside

Some activities can be played outside, for example, in the playground. You may find it refreshing to teach your class outside from time to time if the school's timetable and facilities allow it. One of the advantages of doing some activities, such as *Hopscotch* or *Circle*, in the playground is that you can draw and write with chalk on the ground. Children can draw their own hopscotch court or circle and write words on the surface. If you play inside, you can use string or thin rope and masking tape to shape the hopscotch court or the circle on the floor in the classroom. Numbers and words can be written on paper cards and placed on the floor. Playing outside will probably give you more freedom in the sense that you can worry less about the objects you could break throwing or kicking a ball. When you are in the classroom, you can replace the ball by a softball, bean-bag, or inflatable beach ball that are safer to use and do not make so much noise.

Large classes

Many teachers work with classes of thirty or more learners and so it is more difficult for them to organize the activities in a way to give everyone an opportunity to get involved. Sometimes it is also problematic to provide resources, such as balls or scissors, to everyone in class. It is always a good idea to divide the learners into small groups where they can share the resources and be more active. The teacher can monitor the work in groups and help individual learners. In activities, such as *Modelling clay*, for example, the teacher gives each group a different word to make out of the modelling clay. If you do the activity with a large class and have more groups than words, you can let a few groups work on the same word.

Props and resources

The activities work with resources that are inexpensive and easy to find. Most of them are also reusable so you may find it useful to keep a box or suitcase where you store all the props. In this way you can gradually create a bank of props and resources and use them with different classes and for various activities. Here is a list of resources you may need:

- Balls – tennis balls or a football (for outside); softballs, bean-bags, or inflatable balls (for the classroom)
- Modelling clay – several pieces of modelling clay of different colours in a plastic bag. When you use modelling clay in class, make sure you also bring some sheets of paper to work on. Modelling clay is a little greasy so the learners will need to wash their hands after the activity.
- Jump ropes – several jump ropes made from the elastic string used for sewing, for example, a waistband. Cut 2–3 metres of the string for each jump rope and tie the ends of each piece with a knot. The rope must be elastic and stretchy.
- Toothpicks or safety matches – a box of toothpicks or safety matches. Or you can collect a handful of pine needles outside!
- Marbles – a bag of clay, glass or metal marbles of different colours
- Picture frame – an old picture frame with the backing and glass removed (A3 format) or one made of cardboard paper and decorated using paint, coloured pencils, or markers
- Objects – a set of everyday objects (different sizes, materials, colours, textures)
- String – a set of pieces of string (50cm each)
- Clothes pegs
- Dice
- Coloured pencils or markers
- Chalk
- Scissors
- Masking tape and thin rope or string
- Sticky tape or Blu-tack®

Adapting the activities

Listen and Do is a set of ready-to-use activities that a teacher can immediately follow in class. However, you can also use the material as a springboard and adapt the activities or level them up to better suit your learners, their age group, their interests, what you need to teach or the place where you teach. For example:

- *Parts of the body* teaches vocabulary related to different parts of the body. But you can use the basic idea and adapt the activity to teach any vocabulary set you want.

- Stories in *Storytelling with a piece of string* or in *Gesture and mime* can be kept very simple, or they can be extended.
- Table manners in different cultures can be compared in the activity *At the restaurant*. Do your learners eat with cutlery, silverware, chopsticks or with their hands (then they are probably not allowed to lick their fingers)?
- In *Telephone*, you can use different types of phones, for example, mobile phones, payphones (add words such as 'pick up the handset', 'insert the card/coins', 'collect the card', or 'hang up'), or regular phones with receivers. You may want to pick the one that is most common in the country where you teach. If your students bring their mobile phones to school, let them use their phones as props in the activity.

I hope you and your learners enjoy doing the activities.

Activities

1 Find the small green square

TARGET LANGUAGE   Colours and shapes, prepositions

RESOURCES   Colour paper, scissors

PREPARATION   Cut out paper of different colours, shapes, and sizes such as big and small circles, squares, rectangles and triangles, for example:

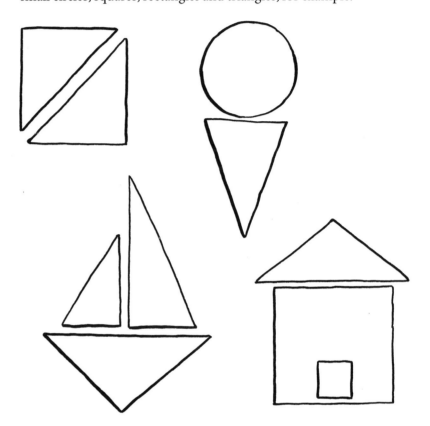

Prepare a set of cut-outs for every pair or small group of learners.

TIME GUIDE   15 minutes+

Activity

1   Let the learners work in pairs or small groups. Give each pair or group a set of colour cut-outs and ask them to spread the shapes on their desk.

2   Play a simple game. Ask the learners to find a particular shape. When they have found it, tell them to put it up. Continue with more examples.

Can you find a triangle?

Can you find the small green square?

Can you find the big blue circle?

Check the shapes and comment on their choices. For example:

Very good. That's the small green square.

That's not a triangle. It's a square. Look, Jan is holding a triangle.

3 Let the learners play with the shapes on the desk. Tell them which shapes they should put together to make new shapes or simple pictures. For example:

a *Find the two small triangles. Can you put them together and make a square? Can you put them together and make a bigger triangle?*

b *Let's make an ice cream. Find the big brown triangle. It's the cone. Now look for the big blue circle. It's blueberry ice cream. Put it on the cone.*

c *Let's find the small green circle and the small brown rectangle. Can you put them together and make a little tree?*

d *Find the two little squares. Put them together. It's your birthday cake. Let's find the small yellow rectangle. It's the candle. Put the candle on the cake.*

e *Let's make a car. Let's find the two little circles. Okay. Now find the big green rectangle. Put the rectangle on the two circles. Let's find the white square. Put the square on the top to make the roof. Good.*

f *Find the big brown triangle. Now find the small white triangle. Put them together and make a brown boat with a white sail. Very good. Let's look for the big blue circle. It's the lake. Put the boat on the lake. Great! Let's find the small red circle. That's the sun. Put it over the lake.*

g *Find the big white square. Okay. Now look for the big brown triangle. Let's put the triangle and the square together and make a nice house. Good. Find the small red square. It's the door. Put it on the big white square. Fine. Let's find the big green rectangle. It's the garden. Put it next to the house. Okay, now we'll find the small blue triangle. That's our swimming pool. Put the swimming pool in the garden. Beautiful!*

2 The train and plane rhyme

TARGET LANGUAGE   'Transport' vocabulary area, Present simple

RESOURCES   Eight flashcards with pictures of Oscar and Sally, the board, sticky tape.

PREPARATION   Copy the pictures on cards. Practise saying the rhyme. Create a suitable space in the classroom for the learners to use during the activity.

TIME GUIDE   15 minutes +

Activity

1 Show a picture of Oscar and Sally and introduce the characters to the learners.

2 Use the flashcards to say the rhyme. When you put up a card, get the learners to mime the means of transport, for example: train – a long line, children hold the shoulders of the person in front of them, plane – children mime the wings of the plane with their arms, car – children mime steering the wheel, bike – children mime holding the handlebars and pedalling, boat – children mime rowing, bus – children mime holding on to the bars when the road is bumpy, horse – children mime riding a horse.

Oscar and Sally

Oscar goes by train	*Sally goes by car*
When it doesn't rain.	*When it is too far.*
Oscar goes by plane	*Sally goes by bike*
When he flies to Spain.	*This is what it's like.*
Oscar goes by boat	*Sally takes a walk*
When he wears his coat.	*When she wants to talk.*
Oscar goes by bus	*Sally rides her horse*
When he visits us.	*In the park, of course.*

3 Ask the learners to line up at one side of the classroom. Use the flashcards and say the rhyme again. Pause after every two lines. Encourage the learners to mime the means of transport and move to the other side of the classroom.

4 Say the rhyme without the flashcards and let the learners mime and move again.

5 Divide the learners into eight groups. Give each group one flashcard. Say the rhyme, two lines at a time, and let the learners with the corresponding picture come to the board. Help them stick the card on the board.

6 Point at the cards on the board. Say the lines and get the learners to guess the rhyming words and mime the actions.

TEACHER	*Oscar goes by…*
LEARNERS	*Train.*
TEACHER	*When it doesn't…*
LEARNERS	*Rain.*

3 Marbles

TARGET LANGUAGE	Colours
RESOURCES	Glass, clay or metal marbles of different colours, spoons – one for each player
	Activity 2: a plastic container for each group of players
PREPARATION	Make or find a suitable space for the activity.
TIME GUIDE	10 minutes + for each activity

Activity 1

1 Ask the learners to make a circle. Give everyone a spoon. Put a red marble on your spoon. Say a word or a simple sentence, for example: 'red' or 'a red marble'. Pass the marble to the next player's spoon. The next player must repeat your sentence and pass the marble to the following player without dropping it and so on.

2 When the first marble gets going, send another marble of a different colour with another message, for example: 'a blue marble'.

3 Send more marbles of different colours along the circle. You can keep the accompanying message very simple, for example, 'a green marble'/'green', or more complex, for example, 'This one is yellow', 'Here comes the pink one', 'Don't lose the white one', etc. In the end all the marbles should come back to you.

Variations

1 Send some marbles in the opposite direction.

2 Ask some learners in the circle to sit down, kneel down, lie down, stand on one leg, etc.

Activity 2

1 Divide the learners into several groups. Give each group a plastic container and put several marbles of different colours in it.

2 Mark a start line at one end of the classroom. Ask the learners to stand behind it in a line. The first learner in each group stands in front of the start line, others stand behind him or her. Place several chairs, one for each group, at the other end of the room.

3 Ask the first learners in the line to play. Give them an instruction to follow. For example: 'Put an orange marble on your spoon'. Let them walk with the marbles on the spoons to their chair, around it, and back to the start line. Count a point for the team whose player crosses the line first. Send the players to the end of the line.

4   The learners in groups take turns to play. Keep changing colours in the instructions, or make the directions more complex. For example:

Put a yellow marble on your spoon.

Put a red marble and a green marble on your spoon.

Put a white, pink and brown marble on your spoon.

Put as many marbles as possible on the spoon.

Close your eyes and pick one marble. What colour is it? Put it on the spoon.

Find a marble that is the colour of the sky. Put it on the spoon.

Put two marbles of the same colour on the spoon.

Put three marbles of different colours on the spoon.

5   Count the points and find the winner.

4 Flowers

TARGET LANGUAGE   Numbers 1–9, 'Flowers' vocabulary area: **grow, the garden, leaves, petals, a long/short/thick/thin stem.**

RESOURCES   The board, a card with a flower for each learner

PREPARATION   Copy the flowers on paper cards, one card for each learner. If you have more learners in class, draw some flowers more than once.

Make enough space in the room for the learners to form a circle.

Practise singing the song 'In my garden' sung to 'Are you sleeping?' (or 'Frère Jacques').

TIME GUIDE   20 minutes +

Activity

1   Draw a flower with several petals and leaves on the board. Invite a few volunteers to come and point at the leaves, petals, and stem. Write the words next to the parts on the board.

2   Tell the learners to make a circle and hold hands. Then ask them to sit down.

3   Give everyone a picture with a flower. Ask the learners to count the number of petals and leaves on their flower.

4   Say, for example, 'In my garden, I grow flowers with five petals'. Get the learners who have flowers with five petals to stand up and hold up their picture.

5   Continue with more examples.

In my garden I grow flowers with   *three petals.*
                                         four leaves.
                                         short/long stems.
                                         thin/thick stems.

6   Ask the learners to put down their cards and stand up. Teach them the song. Get them to repeat the lines after you, move and make simple gestures.

		Examples of movement and gestures
TEACHER	*In my garden,*	The circle moves around.
TOGETHER	*In my garden,*	
TEACHER	*Flowers grow.*	The circle stops moving. The players squat down and then stand up slowly.
TOGETHER	*Flowers grow.*	
TEACHER	*When the wind starts blowing,*	The players move from side to side, like in the wind.
TOGETHER	*When the wind starts blowing,*	
TEACHER	*Petals go.*	The players put up their hands and wiggle
TOGETHER	*Petals go.*	their fingers.
TEACHER	*Two petals go.*	
TOGETHER		The players pretend their fingers are petals. When two petals go, they hide two fingers and show only eight.

7   Start a new round of the song with a different number of petals.

. . . .

Variation   Ask the learners to make a big circle from chairs, one chair fewer than there are players. Stand inside the circle, sing the song together and move around. When you finish singing, each learner tries to sit on a free chair (only one person a chair). The learner who has not found a chair to sit on is out. One chair is taken away from the circle. The game continues until only one learner is left. The last player left is the winner.

5 Fingers

TARGET LANGUAGE   Activity 1: Ordinal numbers – first, second, third, fourth, fifth

Activity 2: Rhyme

RESOURCES   None

PREPARATION   Activity 2: Practise saying the rhyme.

Fingers

The first one said:

Let's go to bed.

The second one said:

Let's play instead.

The third one said:

Let's eat some bread.

The fourth one heard

What said the third.

The little one cried:

Let's go and hide.

TIME GUIDE   5–10 minutes for each activity

Activity 1

1   Invite the learners to play with their fingers. Tell them to show you how they wiggle them, open them wide, make a fist, snap their fingers, etc.

2   Point at your fingers and say: 'my first finger', 'my second finger', 'my third finger', etc. Get the learners to join you and point at their fingers, too.

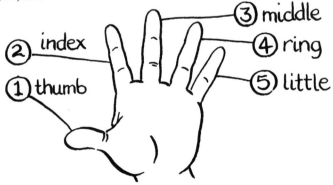

3   Ask the learners to put some fingers together. Say, for example, 'Put the second fingers together', 'Put the fourth fingers together', etc. Make it more difficult by asking them to use a different finger on each hand, for example, 'Put the first finger on your right hand and the fifth finger on your left hand together'.

Activity 2

1   Tell the learners to come and sit in a circle. Say the rhyme. Open your hand, point at your fingers and make simple gestures. Invite the learners to mime with you.

	Examples of mime and gestures
The first one said:	Point at your thumb.
Let's go to bed.	Mime sleeping.
The second one said:	Point at your index finger.
Let's play instead.	Mime playing.
The third one said:	Point at your middle finger.
Let's eat some bread.	Mime eating.
The fourth one heard	Point at your ring finger.
What said the third.	Point at your middle finger.
The little one cried:	Point at your little finger
Let's go and hide.	Make a fist.

2   Practise saying the rhyme. Let the learners do the miming and guess the rhyming words.

TEACHER   *The third one said:*
          Let's eat some…
LEARNERS *Bread.*

6 Have a ball!

TARGET LANGUAGE	Verbs describing what you can do with a ball
RESOURCES	A small ball (a tennis ball or softball) for each player; the board
PREPARATION	Prepare a list of verbs, for example: 'throw', 'catch', 'pass', 'kick', 'head', 'knee', 'hold', 'bounce', etc.
	The activity can be done in the classroom or outside, for example, in the playground. The learners will need some space around. No objects that can be damaged or broken should be close by.
TIME GUIDE	10 minutes + for each activity

Activity 1

1   Ask the learners to stand in a circle. Give everyone a ball. Tell them to listen and do what you say. Start with three verbs.

Throw the ball in the air and catch it like this.

Pass the ball to the person on your left/ right/ in front of you.

2   Add more moves. Continue the activity by calling out the instructions in a random order and giving the learners time to practise doing them.

Bounce the ball against the floor and catch it.	*Knee the ball and catch it.*
Pass the ball to the next person.	*Careful!*
Head the ball and catch it.	*Pick it up and try again.*
Don't lose the ball!	*Well done!*

3   Organize the activity as a game. The ball should always stay close to the player. If someone does a wrong move, loses the ball, or fails to catch it, they leave the circle. These players can start a new circle where they continue playing. The aim of the game is to stay in the first circle as long as possible.

Activity 2

1   Each player has a ball. The players throw the ball in the air, do a simple activity very quickly, and catch the ball again. Make sure the learners have enough space to play and do not hit each other. Make the instructions safe, but challenging. For example:

Throw the ball up and clap your hands three times.

2 Continue the activity by calling out more instructions. For example:

Throw the ball up and   *spin once/twice.*

sit down/ kneel down and stand up.

jump three times.

touch your toes.

stand on one leg.

3 Encourage the learners to think of more actions they could do while the ball is in the air. Write down their suggestions. You can use them when playing next time or with another group of learners.

Variation

The players can also bounce the ball against the ground or wall, do a quick activity, and then catch the ball as it comes back.

7 A walk in the country

TARGET LANGUAGE   'The countryside' vocabulary area: wood, river, path, rain, hill, field, village

RESOURCES   The board

PREPARATION   Draw the picture on the board.

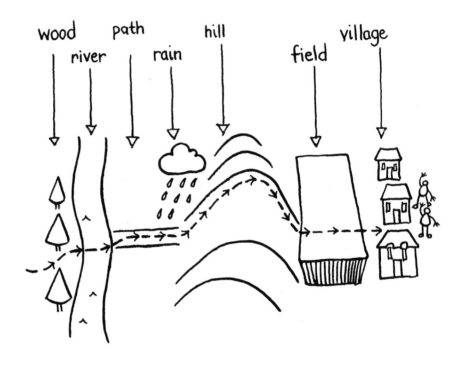

Practise saying the lines:

Through the wood	*One step left, one step right*
Across the river	*Splash, splash, splash, splash*
Along the path	*In the line, in the line*
In the rain	*Stay dry, stay dry*
Over the hill	*Uphill, uphill, downhill, downhill*
Across the field	*Wet, wet, wet, wet*
In the village	*Hello, hello*

Move the desks and chairs to the walls. Use the free space for the activity.

TIME GUIDE   15 minutes +

....

Activity   **1**   Tell the learners you are all going for a walk. Ask them to stand at one end of the classroom.

2   Point at the wood on the board and say, for example:

First we're going through the woods. There are lots of trees there. We don't want to bump into them. Make one step left and then one step right, in a zigzag. *One step left, one step right…* Walk together like that from one end of the classroom to the other, saying: *One step left, one step right …*

3   Point at the river.

Now we're going across the river. There's no bridge. We have to walk across.

Mime walking across the river and splashing the water: *Splash, splash, splash, splash!* Get the learners to repeat the words and walk together across the classroom.

4   Point at the path.

Next we're going along the path. The path is very narrow. We have to walk in a line.

Get the learners to make a line and then walk across the classroom saying: *In the line, in the line …*

5   Point at the rain.

It's raining. We're walking in the rain. Open your umbrellas.

Mime opening the umbrellas. Walk across the room holding the umbrellas and saying: *Stay dry, stay dry…*

6   Point at the hill.

Now we're going over the hill. First we're going uphill. Mime walking on the tips of your toes *and then downhill.* Bend your knees and walk crouching. *Uphill, uphill, uphill, uphill… Downhill, downhill, downhill, downhill…*

7   Point at the field.

Next we're walking across the field. It's been raining. The grass is wet. Lift up your feet. Walk across the field, lifting up your feet, saying *Wet, wet, wet, wet...*

8   Point at the village.

At last we're in the village. There are people standing outside their houses. We're waving at them and saying 'Hello'. Walk across the village and say 'Hello' to everyone.

9   Walk back to the classroom. Follow the same route (village – field – hill – rain – path- river – wood – classroom).

8 Animal walk

TARGET LANGUAGE	Animals, numbers
RESOURCES	A dice for each team of players
PREPARATION	If you do the activity in the classroom, move the desks and chairs to the walls. It can also be played, for example, in the gym or playground.
TIME GUIDE	10 minutes +

Activity

1 Write two sets of numbers 1–6 on the board. Add names or pictures of six different animals next to the first set of numbers. For example:

Animal	Number of stomps, hops, strides, steps
1 frog	1
2 elephant	2
3 mouse	3
4 ostrich	4
5 monkey	5
6 rabbit	6

2 Point to the list of animals. Ask the learners to mime how these animals walk. Do they stomp (heavy steps), hop (all or both feet together) or stride (long steps)? Are their steps long or short, narrow or wide? For example, the frog hops, the elephant stomps with big and wide steps, etc.

3 Mark the start at one end of the classroom and the finish line at the other end. Tell the learners to line up at the start. Roll the dice once and speak to the first learner in the line, for example:

TEACHER   *It's a one.*
Marlies, what's a one?
Point at the list of animals.
MARLIES   *Frog.*
TEACHER   *Yes, it's a frog.*
Roll the dice for the second time.
It's a three.
Hop three times forward like a frog.

The learner makes three hops forward like a frog.

4 Invite the next learner in the line to play. Roll the dice and continue the activity in the same way. The aim of the game is to be the first one to cross the finish line.

5 When the learners become more confident, let them also roll the dice.

Variations

1 Play the game in groups of four or five. The learners in each group take turns to roll the dice and move.

2 Let the learners make their own list of animals.

3 Make the activity more challenging by, for example, using a 12-sided dice or having the list of animals more playful or unusual.

9 Colouring

TARGET LANGUAGE   Colours, the alphabet

RESOURCES   A sheet of paper with the puzzle for each learner, coloured pencils (especially red, blue, green, yellow, and orange), the board

PREPARATION   Copy the puzzle from the picture below on a sheet of paper. Then make a copy for each learner.

Variation: Hand out blank sheets of paper to the learners in class. Let them fold the paper in half and then once again in the same direction. When they unfold the paper, they get four sections to write into. Write the letters in block capitals together as a dictation. Invite a few learners to write the letters on the board.

TIME GUIDE   20 minutes +

Activity

1 Hand out coloured pencils. Let the learners spread them on their desks. Ask them to find some colours and hold up the pencils. For example:

Let's find a blue pencil.

Hold it up like this.

Now put it down.

Have you got a yellow pencil?

2 Give everyone a sheet of paper with the puzzle. Explain that you are going to tell them how to colour these letters. If they colour in all the letters correctly, they will solve the puzzle.

Variation: If the learners wrote the letters in block capitals themselves, tell them to draw a circle around each letter using coloured pencils.

Okay, let's start.

Find the yellow pencil.

Colour in the letter B.

Good. Now pick the green pencil.

3 Continue giving colours of the other letters.

First line: B – yellow, T – green, F – red, S – blue, A – yellow

Second line: S – orange, R – green, I – red, N – yellow, K – blue

Third line: A – yellow, U – orange, R- red, E – green, N – yellow

Fourth line: E – green, N – orange, A – yellow, E – red, Y – blue

4 Let the learners work in pairs or small groups to solve the puzzle. They need to put all the letters of the same colour together to make a word. [Answers: BANANA (yellow), TREE (green), FIRE (red), SKY (blue), SUN (orange)]

5 Write 'Yellow', 'Green', 'Red', 'Blue', and 'Orange' on the board. Ask some learners to write the words from the puzzle next to their colour. Invite the learners to think of more words they link with the colours and write them on the board.

10 Cooking

TARGET LANGUAGE   Vegetables: **onion, garlic, carrot, potato, broccoli, mushroom, peas, beans, salt, pepper**

Cleaning and cutting vegetables: 'peel', 'chop', 'slice', 'cut up into pieces', 'wash'

RESOURCES   Flashcards of vegetables, a big bowl or a paper box

PREPARATION   Copy the pictures below on paper cards. Make a card for each learner in your class. Draw some vegetables more than once if you have more learners.

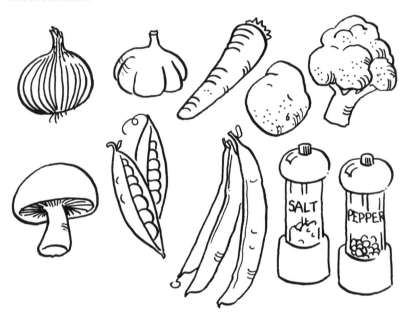

TIME GUIDE   15 minutes +

Activity

1   Invite the learners to come and sit in a circle. Show them the pictures of vegetables, salt and pepper. Hand out the cards, one to each learner.

I went to the market and bought some vegetables. Let's see. I have some carrots. Who wants the carrots?

2   Tell the learners that you are going to cook some vegetable soup together. Explain that you need to clean and cut the vegetables first. Name a vegetable and get the learner holding the picture to put it up. Then mime cleaning or cutting the vegetable together.

We're going to make some soup. But we need to clean and cut the vegetables first.

Where's the onion? Let's peel the onion. Now it's clean. Let's chop it like this.

Continue cleaning and cutting other vegetables.

onion – peel and chop   broccoli – wash and cut up into pieces

garlic – peel   mushroom – wash and slice

carrot – wash and slice   beans – wash

potato – peel and slice   peas – wash

3   Place the big bowl (or the paper box) in the middle of the circle. Say that it is the pot in which you are cooking the soup. Name the vegetables and get the learners to put the pictures in the pot. Then add some salt and pepper.

Let's start cooking. First of all, let's put the chopped onion in the pot. Who has the onion? Put it in the pot. Very good. Where are the sliced carrots? Let's add the carrots. And stir them a little.

4   When all the vegetables and ingredients are in the pot, mime stirring the soup and tasting it.

It smells very good. Mmm, very tasty. I can taste some…(pick one card from the pot) *… garlic.*

5   Invite other learners to mime tasting the soup. Get them to pick one card and say which vegetable or ingredient they can taste.

11 At the restaurant

TARGET LANGUAGE 'Table manners' vocabulary area, prepositions of place

RESOURCES Paper cut-outs of a plate, a spoon, a fork, a knife, a glass, chopsticks, the board, Blu-tack® or another adhesive, a sheet of paper (A4 or letter format) for each learner, markers or pencils

PREPARATION Copy the pictures of the plate, glass, spoon, fork and knife on paper and cut them out with the scissors. Prepare a list of instructions for stage 5.

TIME GUIDE 45 minutes

Activity

1 Write 'plate', 'spoon', 'fork', 'knife', and 'glass' on the board. Take a picture and stick it next to one of the names. Let the learners decide if the name and picture match. Tell them to call out 'OK' if the items match, or shake their head if they do not.

Let's take a picture and stick it here. Is it a glass? No, it isn't.

Let's move the picture. Is it a plate?

2 Draw a big rectangle on the board. Tell the learners that it is a table mat. Use the pictures and get the learners to help you set the table.

We're going to set the table. Here's the plate.

Put the plate in the middle. Where does the fork go?

3   Take off the pictures of the spoon, knife, and fork.

4   Write 'chopsticks' on the board and stick the picture next to the word. Ask the learners to use two pens and practise using chopsticks. Not in every country or culture do people eat with a knife and fork. Where do the chopsticks go on the table set in Japan, for example? (Answer: between the plate and the person). Invite a learner to stick the picture of the chopsticks on the board.

5   Give each learner a sheet of paper and a pencil. The paper is a table mat. Tell the learners to listen and draw the following objects on the mat.

Draw a plate in the middle of the mat.

Draw a knife to the right of the plate.

Draw a spoon next to the knife.

Draw a fork to the left of the plate.

Draw a napkin next to the fork.

Draw a glass in the right corner.

Draw your favourite food on the plate.

Walk around the classroom and ask the learners about their favourite food.

6   Make sure everyone has a drawing in front of them. Explain that you will give them some instructions: good and bad. Tell the learners to listen and mime only the good ones, suitable for eating in a restaurant, for example.

Talk at the table.	*Eat ice cream with the knife.*
Put your feet on the table.	*Talk with your mouth full.*
Pick up the spoon.	*Eat bread with your fingers.*
Eat soup with the spoon.	*Chew the bread.*
Smack your lips.	*Drink some water.*
Pick up the knife and fork.	*Chew with your mouth open.*
Eat your meal with the knife and fork.	

12 Portrait gallery

TARGET LANGUAGE	Present continuous; 'Clothes' and 'Moods' vocabulary areas
RESOURCES	An old picture frame with the backing and glass removed (A3 format). OR One made of cardboard paper decorated using coloured pencils or markers. A set of props, for example, a hat, a scarf, a tie, (sun)glasses, a book, an apple, a doll or teddy bear, a cup or mug, etc.
PREPARATION	Prepare several sets of sentences, describing what a person is wearing, holding, and what he or she feels like.

He/she is wearing sunglasses / a hat / a tie / a scarf, etc.

He/ she is holding an apple / a teddy bear / a book / a hat, etc.

He/she is (very) happy / unhappy / bored / excited / tired / frowning, etc.

TIME GUIDE	20 minutes +

Activity

1   Prepare a chair and a desk in front of the board. Unpack all the props you have brought. While placing the objects on the desk, introduce them briefly to stimulate the learners' interest.

Let's see what we have.   *Look at the…*

This is (a/an)….   *Do you like it?*

And what is this?

2   Sit on the chair. Tell the learners that you want to show them a photo of you. Hold the frame in front of your face so that the learners can see your head in the frame. Describe your mood and what you are wearing and holding in the photo. Use some of the props to create an interesting image in the frame.

I'm wearing my sunglasses. (Pick the sunglasses from the desk and put them on.)

I'm holding a mug. (Pick the mug and hold it within the frame.)

I'm very excited. (Grin broadly)

Do you like the photo?

3   Invite one learner to come to the board and sit on the chair. Describe her photo. For example: 'Marika is wearing a scarf on her head. She is holding an apple. She is frowning.' Repeat the instructions one by one for her to find and use the props and mime the mood. Finally, hold the frame in front of her face. The learner poses while you describe the picture again for the whole class.

4 Continue the activity by inviting more learners to come to the front and mime their photos.

Variations

1 Ask one learner to come to the desk and pick some props. Then invite him or her to sit on the chair, wear/hold the props and mime a mood. Ask questions about his/her portrait, for example, 'Is Tom wearing a tie or a scarf? What is he wearing? Is he holding a teddy bear or a hat? Is he happy or tired?' and get the learners to answer them, or encourage them to describe the portrait using their own sentences.

2 If you can use a camera in class, take photos of the learners' portraits in the frame. Then ask the learners to write captions (words describing or explaining the picture) for the photos and display them in the classroom.

Max on holiday. Wearing a hat and sunglasses. Drinking lemonade. Very happy.

13 Storytelling with a piece of string

TARGET LANGUAGE ‘Clothes’ vocabulary area, prepositions of place, Where are/is my…?

RESOURCES A piece of string (50 cm) for each learner and one for yourself, pictures of the Pirate and the Parrot, cut-outs of the Pirate’s clothes, markers, scissors, sticking tape

PREPARATION Draw the pictures of the Pirate, the Parrot, and the Pirate’s clothes on cardboard paper, cut them out and colour them in. Practise reading the story.

TIME GUIDE 30 minutes +

Activity

1 Give everyone a piece of string. Ask the learners if they can make a knot. Tie a knot on your string and get the learners to make a knot at the end of theirs.

2 Use the pictures to introduce the characters from the story. Describe what the Pirate is wearing. Tell the learners to listen carefully and make a knot for every item of clothing the Pirate and Parrot talk about.

3 Read the story. Make sure you pause while reading to give the learners time to tie their knots.

The Pirate and the Parrot
The Pirate lived on a boat with the Parrot.
One day, when the Pirate was asleep in bed,
the Parrot hid the Pirate’s clothes in different places on the boat.
When the Pirate woke up, he couldn’t find his shoes.
‘Where are my shoes?’ he asked.
‘They are under your pillow.’ said the Parrot.
‘Okay!’ said the Pirate and put on his shoes.
‘Where are my trousers?’ asked the Pirate.
‘They are on the mast.’ said the Parrot.
‘Aha!’ said the Pirate. He ran out to the deck,
pulled the trousers off the mast and put them on.
‘Where is my belt?’ shouted the Pirate.
‘It’s inside the cannon.’ said the Parrot.
‘Fine.’ said the Pirate and put on his belt.

'Where is my scarf?' shouted the Pirate.
'It's on the anchor.' said the Parrot.
'Aha!' said the Pirate and put on his scarf.
'Where is my coat?' shouted the Pirate.
'It's in the treasure chest.' said the Parrot.
'Okay!' said the Pirate, walked back to his cabin and put on his coat.
'Where is my black patch?' asked the Pirate.
'It's in your pocket.' said the Parrot.
'Fine.' said the Pirate and put on his patch.
'Where is my pirate's hat?' asked the Pirate.
'I'm wearing it.' said the Parrot.
'Okay.' said the Pirate.
'And where are you?' asked the Pirate.
'I'm in the kitchen. I'm making you a cup of tea.' said the Parrot.

4   Tell the learners to count the knots they have made. Check their numbers (Answer: 7; shoes, trousers, belt, scarf, coat, patch, hat). Then ask them to untie the knots.

5   Tell the story again. Use the pictures and a lot of gestures to make the meaning clear. Put up the pictures of the Pirate and the Parrot every time they speak in the story. When you get to the lines where the Pirate asks about his clothes, pause for a while, get the learners to use the string and tie it around the part of the body where the item is worn (shoes–feet, trousers–legs, belt–waist, etc.). You can tie your string around the Pirate's picture.

6   Draw the pictures of the boat and the Pirate's cabin on the board. Stick the pictures of the Pirate and the Parrot, and the cut-outs of the Pirate's clothes, at the side. Read the story again and invite the learners to stick the cut-outs to the places where the Parrot hid the clothes.

14 Toothpicks

TARGET LANGUAGE	Vocabulary revision, spelling
RESOURCES	Toothpicks or matches (five toothpicks or matches for each learner), the board, paper and pencils
PREPARATION	Activity 1: Prepare a list of objects or animals the learners can make using toothpicks
TIME GUIDE	10 minutes + for each activity

Activity 1

1 Divide the learners into pairs. Give each pair ten toothpicks. Draw, for example, a house using six simple lines on the board. Ask the learners to make a similar house using the toothpicks on their desks.

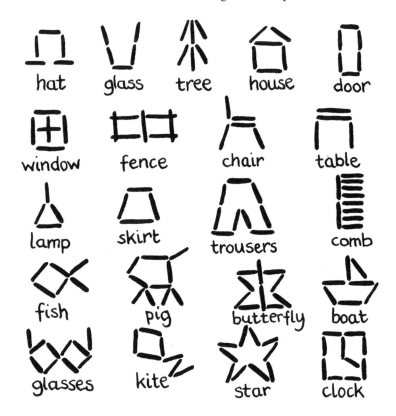

2 Use the list of words you have prepared and ask the learners to make the things or animals from the toothpicks. When they create more complex shapes, you may invite them to look at each other's work.

3 Ask the pairs to use their imagination and make a picture of another thing or animal using the toothpicks. Then invite the learners to stand up, walk around the class, and guess what the pictures the other pairs have created represent.

Activity 2

1   Tell the learners to try out which letters of the alphabet they can make using the toothpicks.

2   Put the learners into groups of four. Which words (or sentences) can they make using the toothpicks they have? Give each group a sheet of paper and pencil to record the words.

3   Ask each group to pick a word from their list for the other groups to make.

15 Circle

TARGET LANGUAGE	Time expressions and numbers
RESOURCES	Chalk (or cards and a marker)
PREPARATION	Find a suitable space for the activity. Draw several circles on the ground with chalk, or let the learners draw them. You need one circle for each small group of players. (You can also use 12 paper cards with numbers written on them. Spread them on the floor and make a circle.)
TIME GUIDE	10 minutes +

Activity

1   Put the learners into small groups. Draw a circle for each group and divide it into twelve sections like this:

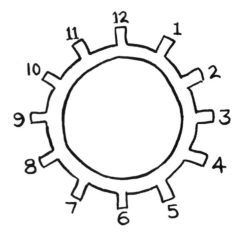

2   Ask the learners to stand around their circle. The circle acts as a counter that goes up to 12 or as a clock. Give the learners simple instructions. They should listen and move to the right number on the circle to give the answer. Get the learners to move every time the number changes. For example:

a *Four plus one.*

b *Seven minus three.*

c *I bought six oranges. On my way home I dropped two. Then I gave one to a friend. I ate two. How many oranges do I have now?*

d *I got a box with twelve chocolates. I ate a chocolate on Monday, two on Tuesday, three on Wednesday and two on Thursday. How many chocolates do I still have?*

e *I went for a trip around Europe. I started in January and went to France for a month. Then to Germany for two months, Holland for two weeks and Belgium for two weeks. What month is it now?*

f   *I was born in December, my sister in March, my father in May and my mother in October. Which month were you born?*

g   *At six o'clock I have dinner for one hour. Then I watch TV for two hours. I read a book for an hour. What time do I go to bed?*

h   *We start at nine o'clock. We have an English lesson for an hour and then maths for two hours. When do we have lunch?*

3   Encourage the learners to play on their own in the groups. They can give each other simple directions, for example, six plus three, ten minus five, etc. and use the circle to respond to them.

16 Clothes pegs

TARGET LANGUAGE	Rooms in a house, 'furniture' vocabulary area
RESOURCES	Clothes pegs, paper, markers
PREPARATION	Make play-boards out of paper. Draw several boxes on the sheet. Write one name of a room or place around the house in each box. Make a copy for each learner. OR Draw the play-board on the board. Hand out paper and markers and let the learners copy it on their sheets of paper.

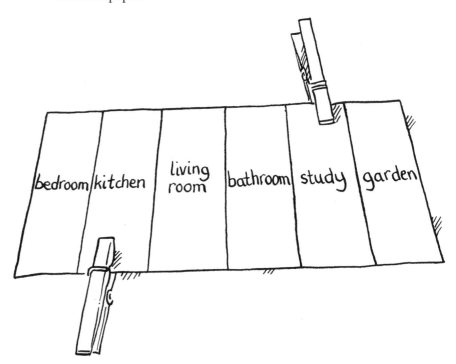

TIME GUIDE	5–10 minutes for each activity

Activity 1

1 Give each learner a board with the names of rooms and some clothes pegs.

2 Ask the learners simple questions, for example, 'Where can you find a fridge?' Get them to clip the pegs on the box with the room where they can usually find the item, for example, 'kitchen'. Sometimes more than one answer is possible, for example: 'Where can you find windows?'

3 Let them compare their boards in pairs, then check the answers.

4 Continue asking about other items, for example, a desk, a cooker, plants, a sofa, a lamp, a carpet, etc.

Activity 2

1   Let the learners play a game. Tell them to listen to a simple story, figure out which rooms you talk about and then put the clothes-pegs on the right boxes. The winner is the first person who puts pegs on all the rooms mentioned in the story. For example:

a   *It's Sunday morning. Everyone is at home. My brother is sleeping. My sister is having a bath. My mother is cooking lunch. My father is cutting the grass, and my grandma is watching TV.*

b   *One day I was looking for my teddy bear. First I looked under the bed. Next I checked the laundry basket next to the bath. Then I looked inside the cupboard where we keep sweets and chocolate. Last I looked under the big pillow on the sofa. Hurrah! My teddy was there!*

c   *Next week we are going shopping. We need some new things for the house. First we need to buy some new plates and spoons. We are also looking for a new computer. Then we want to buy a new bath mat.*

Variation

Write your own stories for the game to level the activity to your class and practise the language you need to focus on.

17 Hopscotch

TARGET LANGUAGE	A set of words the learners are familiar with
RESOURCES	A marker for each group of players, for example, a stone or pen; chalk (or rope, masking tape, and paper cards)
PREPARATION	The activity works best if played on the surface where you can draw with chalk on the ground. The hopscotch court can also be made on the floor using rope, masking tape, and paper cards for pictures or words.
	Prepare sets of words for the squares or sections, for example, clothes: coat, shoes, socks, T-shirt, dress, hat, skirt, scarf.
TIME GUIDE	10 minutes + for each activity

Activity 1

1 Use some chalk and draw a large rectangle on the ground. Divide it into 8–10 sections. Write one word into each section, or ask the learners to write them. For example:

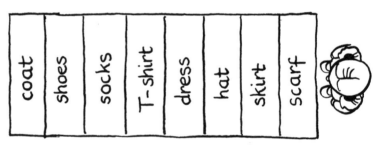

2 Ask the learners to stand at one side of the court. Call out a word, for example 'dress'. Tell them to walk or run across the court, jumping over the square with the word and stepping on the rest of them. Make the activity more challenging by calling two words at the same time.

Activity 2

1 Draw a hopscotch court on the ground. Write a word into each square.

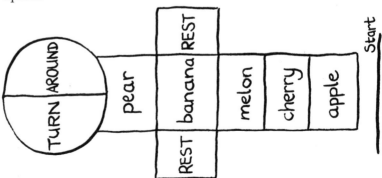

2 Ask the learners if they know how to play hopscotch. Encourage a volunteer to show how to hop in or over the squares, or demonstrate the activity yourself. Comment on what you are doing. For example:

Stand behind the line. Toss the marker. It must land in the first square.

You mustn't step in the square where the marker is.

Hop over 'Apple' to 'Cherry'. Just on one leg. Say the name of the square where you land. Then hop to 'Melon'. Next, ' Banana'.

Now jump to 'Rest', each leg on one side like this. Then 'Pear' on one foot again.

Next jump to 'Turn around' with both feet. Turn around.

Now hop back: 'Pear!', 'Rest!', 'Banana!', 'Melon!', 'Cherry!'

In 'Cherry', pick up the marker from 'Apple'. Hop to 'Apple' and out.

If you made no mistakes, you can toss the marker again.

Now it must land in the second square.

3 Let the learners play. If a player steps on the line, misses a square, or loses balance, his or her turn ends. When he or she plays again, the player starts where he or she last left off. The first player to complete one course for every square on the court wins the game.

Variations

1 Use drawings instead of words in the squares.

2 Let the learners play the game in groups of three or four. Ask each group to draw their own hopscotch. Give each team a different set of words to write inside. Later on, you can rotate the teams and let them hop in the other courts.

3 Write simple directions into the squares, for example: 'Clap!' 'Kneel!' 'Wiggle!' Get the players to carry out the instructions as they land in the squares. Other team members can call out the directions for the player when hopping in the court.

18 Blindfold walk

TARGET LANGUAGE	Giving directions: Take one step forward, Turn left/right, Stop!
RESOURCES	Board, scarf
PREPARATION	None
	This activity is described for the classroom. A playground or hall are also suitable.
TIME GUIDE	20 minutes+

Activity

1   Ask the class to help you move the desks and chairs to the walls to create a space in the middle. For example:

We need some more space today.

Can you help me move the desks and chairs?

Let's be quiet.

2   Invite the learners to come and stand in the middle of the room. Make sure everyone has enough space around them. Give simple directions and move yourself. Tell the learners to follow you. For example:

Take	one		forward	
	two	step/s	back	
	three		to the	left
				right

Turn	left			
	right			
	around			
	Stop!			

backwards

to the right

turn around

3 Elicit from the learners which instructions they remember and ask them to show what they mean. Help with the language and write their suggestions on the board.

4 Ask a confident student to give directions to the rest of the class.

5 Put the class into small groups and tell them to take turns giving directions.

6 Tell the class to stand at random in the middle of the classroom. You stand at one end. Explain to the class that you are going to cover your eyes with a scarf and they have to guide you to the other end of the room – without bumping into anyone. Cover your eyes with the scarf and follow the class' instructions.

19 Gestures and mime

TARGET LANGUAGE
Action verbs, for example: write, laugh, play, cook, swim, phone, sleep, speak, break, catch, drink, eat, read, sit, give, open, carry, etc.

RESOURCES
The board

PREPARATION
Activity 2: Prepare slips of paper with short messages written on them, for example: 'eat spaghetti', 'catch a ball', 'break a window', 'drink tea', 'give a present', 'carry a bag', 'open a window', 'play the guitar', etc.

Activity 3: Prepare a simple story or text and practise reading it.

TIME GUIDE
5–10 minutes for each activity

Activity 1

1   Write two or three action verbs on the board. Ask the learners to add more verbs. Write their suggestions on the board.

2   Make a circle. Say a verb from the list on the board, for example, 'drink' and make a gesture that explains the activity, for example, mime drinking water out of a glass.

3   Invite the learner standing next to you to say 'Drink' and mime your gesture. Then he or she adds another verb, for example 'break', and make a new gesture, for example, miming breaking a stick into two pieces.

4   The next learner says and mimes the previous two words and adds a new one, etc. The learner who breaks the chain by leaving out some words starts a new round.

Activity 2

1   Divide the learners into two teams. Ask a learner from the first team to come to the board. Give the learner a slip of paper with a short message written on it, for example, 'eat spaghetti'. Tell him or her to use gestures and mime the meaning of the message. The first team have to guess what the activity is. Count a point for a correct answer.

Evelien, please come to the board.

Here's a slip of paper.

Read the message. Is it clear?

Don't say what it is, but mime it.

Your team have to guess.

2 Invite a learner from the other team to mime the next message. Now the other team try and guess the activity. Again count a point for a correct answer.

3 Invite other learners from the teams to mime more messages. In the end add up the points to see which team have been more successful at miming and guessing.

Activity 3

1 Prepare a short text. Read it sentence by sentence. Tell the learners to listen and make as many gestures as possible to illustrate the meaning of each sentence. Encourage them to stand up and move around the classroom while listening to the story.

I read a book last night. Suddenly I heard the bell ring. I went downstairs and opened the door. It was very cold outside, but there was no-one there. I closed the door and walked to the kitchen. I opened the fridge and pulled out a bottle of milk. I opened the bottle and drank some milk. Then I put the milk back to the fridge and closed the door. Suddenly I heard the bell again. I opened the door. What a surprise! There was a small cat there. I let her in and closed the door. Then I went to the kitchen and poured some milk into a bowl. I gave it to the cat. She began drinking the milk.

20 Hit the answer

TARGET LANGUAGE   Activity 1: 'Jobs' vocabulary area, Present simple
Activity 2: Time expressions

RESOURCES   Activity 1: Two softballs or bean bags, the board, chalk
Activity 2: A small ball for each group of players

PREPARATION   Activity 1: Prepare a list of jobs and their definitions. For example:

a mechanic – works in a garage, repairs cars
a doctor – works in a hospital, treats sick people
a pilot –sits in a cockpit, flies a plane
a secretary – works in an office, types letters, makes phone calls
a vet – works in an animal hospital, treats sick animals
a chef – works in a kitchen/restaurant, cooks food
a farmer– works outside, grows crops, keeps animals

Activity 2: The activity works best if played on the surface where learners can write with chalk on the ground. But they can also write on paper cards and then spread them on the floor.

TIME GUIDE   10 minutes + for each activity

....

Activity 1

1   Draw eight squares on the board and write a name of a job in each of them.

2   Invite a volunteer to the board. Give him or her a small ball or a bean bag. Pick one of the eight jobs and describe what the person does. Tell the learner to find the word for the job on the board and hit it with the ball or the bag. Keep on adding information to the definition until the learner finds the target word.

It's a person who works outside … often in the field …where he or she grows crops … such as potatoes or vegetables … or keeps animals … for example, cows or sheep.

3   Then invite other learners to the board to play. Describe other jobs from your list. Let two learners play at the same time. You can make the activity into a simple game. Whoever hits the right word first is the winner.

4 Make the definitions more general so that they can apply to more jobs. Ask other learners in class to judge if the answers are correct.

It's a person who   *wears a uniform.*

studied at university.

works indoors.

works with people.

can type.

sits most of the time.

Activity 2

1 Divide the learners into small groups. Give each group some chalk. Dictate a set of words, for example, the days of the week. The learners take turns and write the words on the ground. Then they draw a big circle around them.

2 Tell the groups to stand around their circles. Give one learner from each group a small ball. Describe one of the words from the circle using a simple sentence. Ask the players to bounce the ball against the word which they think is the correct answer. The other learners try to catch the ball. For example:

today	*the day when you don't go to school*
tomorrow	*the day before Wednesday*
yesterday	*the day between Friday and Sunday*
the day after tomorrow	*May the twentieth*

3 Check the answer. The learner who has caught the ball plays in the next round.

21 Modelling clay

TARGET LANGUAGE	The alphabet, spelling
RESOURCES	A piece of modelling clay and a sheet of paper for each learner
PREPARATION	Prepare a list of words. If the learners work, for example, in groups of four, you should use words with four letters such as: 'name' 'cold', 'four', 'long', 'what', 'have', etc.
	Prepare a list of simple instructions that the learners can carry out, for example: 'Touch your ears', 'Sit on the floor', 'Stand on one leg', etc.
TIME GUIDE	15 minutes +

Activity

1   Give everyone a piece of modelling clay and a sheet of paper to work on. Play with the clay and talk about how it feels.

How does it feel?

Can you squeeze it?

Is it soft or hard?

2   Let the learners roll balls, 'snakes', and 'snails' from the clay.

Make a small ball.

Roll it into a snake.

Coil it up and make a snail's shell.

3   Ask the learners to roll a long snake and use it to make one letter of the alphabet. Any letter they like. How many learners have made the same letter?

4   Divide the class into groups of four. Use your list and give the groups a word. The groups must decide which letters they need to make to spell the word correctly. Each learner makes one letter. Then they put the letters together to spell the word. Use other words from the list and let the learners make them.

5   Use one of the simple instructions from your list. For example, 'Stand on one leg'. Give each group one word from the sentence to work on. If you teach a big class, have more groups to work on the same word. When the learners have made their words, ask them to stand up, walk around the classroom and see the words the other groups have created. Let them combine the words together and guess what the instruction is. Then get them to mime it. Let the groups work on more instructions from the list.

Variations

1   Use the clay to make numbers.

    a   Practise reading two-or three-digit numbers or years

    b   Make up simple equations with mistakes in them, for example: '7 + 4 = 12'. Let the learners find the mistakes and correct them by re-shaping some of the digits. Encourage them to say what is not correct and how they are going to change it.

2   Divide the learners into pairs, A and B. Tell A to close their eyes. Write a word on the board for B, for example, 'key' and then wipe it off. Tell A to open their eyes and ask B to make the object out of the clay. A has to guess what the object is. Then they change the roles. You can experiment with abstract words, such as 'love', 'smile', and 'song', and let the learners use their imagination and clay to depict them.

22 Objects

TARGET LANGUAGE	Adjectives, prepositions: on, under, in, to, etc.
RESOURCES	A set of objects, for example: ball, teddy bear, umbrella, spoon, cup, apple, potato, pen, candle, comb, torch, belt, scarf, toothbrush, socks, etc.
PREPARATION	Prepare at least twice as many objects as you have learners in the class
TIME GUIDE	10 minutes +

Activity 1

1 Put a few desks together at the back of the classroom and place the objects on them.

2 Divide the learners into two groups. Each group forms a line. Ask the first learner in each line to pick one object from the desks, for example, 'Go back to the desks and bring something soft'. When they bring the objects, have a short conversation about their choice. Then ask the learners to put the objects back and go stand at the end of the line.

Let's see.

What is it?

Is it (soft)?

Hold it. / Touch it.

3 Ask the next two learners to pick another object. The activity goes on like this as you change adjectives in the instructions. You can ask the learners to bring objects which are, for example, 'small', 'heavy', 'light', 'interesting', 'long', 'cheap', 'expensive', 'black', 'useful', etc.

Variation

Make the directions more specific by comparing the object you want them to pick with another object, for example, 'Bring something lighter than this umbrella'. You can let them hold the other object before they make their choice.

Activity 2

1 Ask one learner from each team to go to the desks and bring back one object they like.

2 Tell the learners what to do with their objects. Get them to carry one instruction each. For example:

Give the apple to someone else.

Put the teddy bear on the chair.

Hide the ball in someone's bag.

Put the pen in your pocket.

Drink out of the cup.

Switch the torch on.

Put the scarf over the torch.

Open up the umbrella.

Put the belt on.

3 Ask the next two learners to pick new objects.

Variation

Organize the activity as a competition between the two groups. Count a point for each instruction the teams have performed correctly. In the end add up the points to find the winner.

23 Parts of the body

TARGET LANGUAGE Parts of the body, **Can you…?**

RESOURCES A sheet of paper and a pair of scissors for each learner, markers, the board

PREPARATION Draw the lines and words from the chart on a sheet of paper (A4 or letter format) with a black marker. Copy the drawing for each learner. OR Draw the chart on the blackboard, hand out blank sheets of paper and markers to the learners and ask them to copy it.

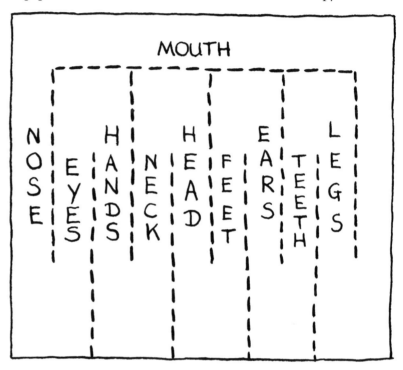

TIME GUIDE 20 minutes+

Activity

1 Hold a blank sheet of paper and a pair of scissors. Ask the learners if they can cut a hole in this paper big enough for them to walk through. Tell them you have 10 riddles. If they answer them all, they can see how to cut such a hole.

2 Make sure everyone has a sheet of paper with the chart and a pair of scissors.

3 Read the following riddles to the learners, one by one. Ask them to look for the answer to each riddle in the chart. When they find the word, tell them to cut the whole line the word is written along with the scissors. The first line is more difficult to cut than the other ones. The learners have to make a little hole in the paper with the scissors first, and then start cutting along the line.

You can smell with it.   *You can think with it.*

You can kiss or eat with it.   *You can see with them.*

You can walk with them.   *You can bite with them.*

You can write with them.   *You can turn your head with it.*

You can hear with them.   *You can kick the ball with them.*

4   When the learners answer all the riddles and cut the lines in the sheet, they can stretch the paper apart carefully and walk through the hole.

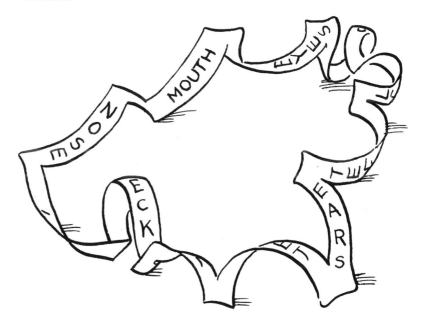

5   Let the learners play with the paper chain. Ask them simple questions and see if they can do it.

Can you walk through it?

Can you hold it in your hand?

Can you hold it round your neck?

Can you hold it on your ears?

Can you hold it in your teeth?

6   If the learners are confident to ask questions, you can let them walk around the classroom and ask each other what they can do with the paper chain. For example:

LEARNER 1   *Can you hold it on your finger?*

LEARNER 2   *Yes, I can.* (Learner 2 shows Learner 1 how he can hold the paper chain on his finger.)
                      Can you hold it on your nose?

LEARNER 1   *Yes, I can!*

24 Rope jumping

TARGET LANGUAGE   Prepositions

RESOURCES   Jump ropes – one rope for every three or four learners

PREPARATION   Make the jump ropes from the elastic string used for sewing, for example a waistband. The rope must be elastic and stretchy. Cut 2–3 metres of the string for each jump rope and tie the ends of each piece with a knot.

TIME GUIDE   15 minutes +

Activity

1   Divide the class into groups of three or four. Give each group a jump rope. Two learners ('enders') in each group stand opposite each other. They put the jump rope around their ankles and stretch it. The other member or members ('jumpers') stand between them, close to the rope.

2   Demonstrate a simple routine with one pair. Say the instructions loud and jump yourself. Encourage one jumper in each group to do the routine with you using their rope. For example:

Stand on one side of the rope. Jump inside.

Open and close your legs three times. Stretch the rope like this. One, two, three.

Step on the rope.

Jump outside the rope.

Turn over and face the rope.

Jump to the other side. Take the rope with your shoes and cross it.

Walk back and stretch the other side of the rope.

Step on the rope.

Lift your toes and let the rope go. Well done!

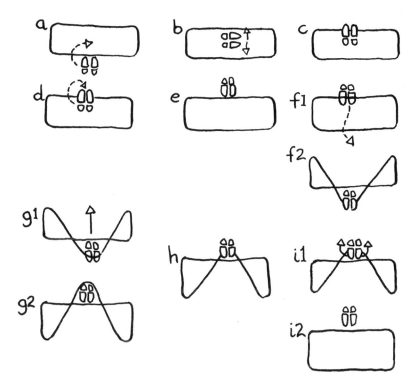

3   Tell the jumpers to exchange their places with one of the enders in their group. Ask the enders to raise the rope one level up (from the ankles to the middle of the leg, between knees and ankles). Give the jumpers the directions step by step and do the routine. If necessary, demonstrate some of the steps yourself again.

4   The jumper in each group changes their place with the ender who has not jumped yet. Raise the rope to another level (knees). Give the directions step by step and do the routine one more time.

5   Do the activity as a competition between the groups. Continue giving the directions. Do several routines at different levels (ankles, the middle of the leg, knees). Let the learners in each group take turns and jump. Count a point for the group if their jumper makes a mistake, for example, does not step on the rope or loses it. In the end add up the points. The team with the fewest points are the winners.

Variations

1   Change the width of the rope, not only its height. The players can stand in a wide stance, or place the rope only on one leg.

2   Ask the groups to make up their own routine and prepare their sets of directions. Let the groups perform their new routines to each other.

25 The morning routine

TARGET LANGUAGE   'Morning routine' vocabulary area

RESOURCES   The board

PREPARATION   Draw the picture on the board.

tap
toothbrush
hairbrush
mirror
towel

TIME GUIDE   20 minutes

Activity

1 Read the five words from the picture: 'tap', 'toothbrush', 'hairbrush', 'mirror', 'towel'. Ask individual learners to come to the board and write the words next to the arrows. Once they have written the word in the picture, wipe it off the list.

2 Pretend that you have just woken up in the morning. Mime opening the door to the bathroom and stand beside the picture. Say a sentence from the list of morning activities below. Use the picture and mime the activity. Then write the sentence down on the board. Point at the sentence, read it, and get the learners to mime what it means. Then move on to the next sentence.

Turn on the tap.   *Dry your hands.*

Wash your face.   *Brush your hair.*

Brush your teeth.   *Look in the mirror.*

Turn off the tap.

3 Read the sentences one after another and let the learners mime them.

4 Play a game with the learners. Use the sponge and wipe one object off the picture, for example, the towel. It means that they must not mime any actions that involve using the towel. Read the sentences from the list, one at a time. Ask the learners to repeat the sentence after you and mime it. When you get to talk about drying hands, they repeat the sentence, but they must not do the miming. Continue wiping off further objects from the drawing.

TEACHER *Turn off the tap.*
LEARNERS *Turn off the tap.* (Mime turning off the tap)
TEACHER *Dry your hands.*
LEARNERS *Dry your hands.* (No miming)

5 Write the following pairs of words on the board. Invite two volunteers to join you. Read out the pairs and let each learner mime one phrase.

turn on the tap — turn off the tap

brush your teeth — rinse your teeth

wash your hands — dry your hands

dry your hair — brush your hair

6 Divide the learners into pairs and tell them to stand opposite each other in two lines like this.

A
↓ ○ ○ ○ ○ ○
↑ ○ ○ ○ ○ ○
B

Each A learner thinks of an activity from the list of pairs. He or she mimes it and says what it is, for example 'brush your hair'. The B learners then mime the other activity in the pair and say what it is, for example, 'dry your hair'. Then the roles change.

26 Telephone

TARGET LANGUAGE   'Telephone' vocabulary area, numbers

RESOURCES   Board, a call card for each learner, a paper phone (or a real phone), paper and pencils

PREPARATION   Make a paper phone (or bring a real one). Make call cards. Write the 'Chain call chant' on the board.

Chain call chant

Pick up the phone.

Dial the number.

Press the call key.

Make the call.
(Hello, this is…, Bye.)

Press the 'End' key.

Put down the phone.

Call cards

Make as many cards as there are learners in class and one for yourself. Each card has two numbers. The first one belongs to the card holder. The other number, with the picture of the phone, is the one to dial. The numbers create a chain. The number to dial on one card is the card holder's number on the next. For example:

894 301 📞 350 673	350 673 📞 248 019	248 019 📞 676 239
676 239 📞 980 654	980 654 📞 175 716	175 716 📞 269 389

TIME GUIDE   20 minutes

Activity

1 Invite the learners to come and sit in a circle.

2 Show them your phone, or draw a picture of it on the board. Give everyone a strip of paper and tell them to draw their own phone.

3 Read the directions from the 'Chain call chant' from the board. Use the phones and mime them together.

4 Give the directions again. This time encourage the learners to perform them on their own.

5 At random, give everyone a call card. Keep one yourself. Show the learners which number on the card is theirs and which number they will call.

6 Stand in the middle of the circle. Start the chain call chant. Get the learners to repeat the lines after you and mime the instructions. When you dial the number, the learners need to listen carefully to see whether the number was theirs. If there is no answer, repeat the number as many times as necessary. The learner whose number has been called has to say 'Hi, this is…'. He or she then starts a new round of the chant.

7 The teacher and the learner whose number has been called exchange their places. The teacher sits down on the chair. The learner stands in the middle.

8 Now the learner says the chant and calls the number on his or her card. The other learners repeat the lines after him or her, use their phones and mime the instructions. The chant goes on until all the numbers have been called.

27 Trading

TARGET LANGUAGE **Can we have …?, Please give us …**
Can we see…?, Please show us …

RESOURCES A set of 12 mime cards, the board

PREPARATION Make 12 mime cards. Write numbers 1–12 on one side of the cards and the instructions on the other. The cards are 'weighted'. The cards with lower scores are easier to mime than the higher ones that are more embarrassing or difficult to perform.

1   *Wiggle your ears.*

2   *Shut and open one eye.*

3   *Take off your shoes and put them on again.*

4   *Touch the floor, but don't bend your knees.*

5   *Turn around five times and then walk straight on.*

6   *Mime eating a very sour lemon.*

7   *Draw a circle with one hand and a square with the other.*

8   *You are a group of ballet dancers. Show us your best dance.*

9   *Mime fish swimming in a fishbowl.*

10   *Sing La-da-da-di-da pretending to be an opera singer.*

11   *You are clowns in the circus. Make us laugh doing pantomime.*

12   *Run round the classroom pretending to be a chicken.*

TIME GUIDE 30 minutes

Activity

1   Divide the class into four teams. Ask the teams to pick their names. Write numbers from 1–12 on the board.

2   Tell the teams that you have a set of twelve mime cards. They can win a different number of points for each card. The cards with low scores are easier to mime than the cards with higher scores that have more difficult or embarrassing instructions. The teams have to decide in each round if they want to play it safe or take a risk. The aim of the game is to win the most points.

3   Decide in which order the teams play.

4   Ask the first team to pick a card. Cross out the number they have chosen on the board.

Read the instruction and let the team play.

TEACHER *Dolphins, it's your turn to trade.*
DOLPHINS *Please give us number 6.*
TEACHER *OK. (Crosses out the number on the board.)*
Number Six. Mime eating a very sour lemon.

5 Once they mime the instruction, give them the card. It is the next team's turn to pick a number.

6 When you have crossed all the numbers on the board, the teams can start trading the cards between each other. Ask one team to hold up all their cards. The other teams should see their numbers. Invite the following team to pick one of them. Ask the first team to read out the instruction from the back of the card. If the other team mimes the instruction, they get the card. Then they hold up all their cards for the next team to pick from.

DOLPHINS   *Jaguars, can you show us your cards?*
JAGUARS   (Hold the cards so that the other team can see the numbers)
DOLPHINS   *Please give us number 7.*
JAGUARS   *OK.* (One learner reads out the instructions from the card)

7 When you complete the round and all the teams have four cards again, ask them to add up the numbers and count their scores.

28 Housework

TARGET LANGUAGE 'Household jobs' vocabulary area, Present continuous

RESOURCES The board, pieces of paper for Game 2

PREPARATION Write the substitution table on the board.

Action	Object	with	Tool
sweep	the plants		the watering can
wash	the meal		the cloth
water	the dishes		the broom
cook	the floor		the spoon
wipe	the table		the towel
dry			

TIME GUIDE 30 minutes +

Activity

1 Read the verbs from the table and get the learners to mime what they mean. Invite a few volunteers to the board to draw lines between the verb and words from the other two columns. (Answers: sweep the floor with the broom, wash the dishes with the cloth, water the plants with the watering can, cook the meal with the spoon, wipe the table/ floor with the cloth, dry the dishes/table with the towel)

2 Divide the learners into pairs, A and B. Give each A an activity from the list to mime. Tell B to walk around the classroom and ask one A about what he or she is doing. B starts miming the household job and A walks away to ask other learners about what they are doing. The activity then continues in the same manner.

LEARNER B *What are you doing?*
LEARNER A *I'm watering the plants.*
LEARNER B (Starts miming the household job.)
LEARNER A (Leaves B to talk to someone else.)

3 Game 1: Invite the learners to make a circle and play a game. Stand in the middle of the circle, point at a learner and say a name of a tool, for example, 'Broom!' The learner must start miming sweeping and say 'Sweep with the broom!' as soon as possible. If the learner makes a mistake, hesitates too long or starts miming another activity, he or she must replace you in the centre. The learner then points at another player and names a tool, and so on.

4 Game 2: Prepare small pieces of paper. Divide them into three piles. Ask the learners to write some verbs on the pieces in the first pile, some objects in the second pile, and some tools in the third pile. Then fold up all the pieces so that nobody can see the words. Mix the folded bits in the piles. Invite a learner at a time to pick one piece from each pile, for example 'dry', 'the meal', 'the towel', make a sentence out of the words, 'dry the meal with the towel', and try to mime the activity. Some combinations may be so unusual that it may be very difficult to act them out.

29 Sentences

TARGET LANGUAGE	Past tenses, **was/were**, word order
RESOURCES	Ten paper cards, a marker, clothes-pegs or paper-clips, the board
PREPARATION	Write the following words and punctuation symbols on the cards:

Where, were, wasn't, you, I, last night, on the moon, ?, .

Prepare a list of sentences (both statements and questions) that can be made up from the words.

TIME GUIDE	10 minutes +

Activity

1 Make sure you have enough space for ten learners to mingle. Invite ten volunteers to join you. Randomly give the learners numbers 1–10. Play a simple number game. Say, for example, 'One plus three plus four equals …'. Get the learners with numbers one, three, and four line up and then the learner with number eight has to join the end. Continue the activity with more sentences.

2 Use clothes pegs or paper clips to attach the word cards to the front of the learners' clothes. Read the word for each learner. Briefly check if everyone remembers their word.

Notice the difference between 'where' /weə/ and 'were' /wɜː/.

3 Ask the learners to stand at the side of the mingling space. Say a sentence, for example, 'I was on the moon'. The learners who hear their word should come to the middle. They line up to make the sentence. Repeat the sentence as many times as necessary. Ask other learners to check the order. Invite them to move the learners to rearrange the order if necessary.

4   Give the learners more sentences to make:

Where were you?

Where was I?

Were you on the moon?

I wasn't on the moon.

You weren't on the moon.

Last night I was on the moon.

You weren't on the moon last night.

••

Variation

When the learners line up, ask them to hold hands. The first and the last person in the line also come together to hold hands and the whole group makes a circle. They should face the outside so that other learners can read their cards. Then the circle starts moving clockwise. The viewers read the sentence as it moves.

30 The magic wand

TARGET LANGUAGE   Places and prepositions of place

RESOURCES   A magic wand, the board, paper

PREPARATION   Make a magic wand, for example, from a wooden stick or a piece of dry branch. Decorate it using markers or wrap it up in coloured paper.

Prepare several slips of paper – one for each group of players. Write a name of a place on each of them.

Find or make a suitable space for the activity. Children will need some space to move around.

TIME GUIDE   15 minutes +

Activity

1 Show the learners the magic wand. Tell them that the wand has the power to take them to any place they can imagine. Write names of a few places on the board and pre-teach the words the learners are not familiar with. For example:

in space	*in the shower*
in the circus	*on the beach*
on horseback	*in the jungle*
at the tennis match	*on the trampoline*
at the funfair	*at the party*
in the playground	*in the kitchen*

2 Ask the learners to walk around the classroom and listen. Wave the magic wand and call out a name of a place and 'Abracadabra!' When the learners hear the name of the place, they should start doing or miming activities typical of such a location. They stay there until you call out a new name.

3 Divide the learners into small groups. Hand each group a paper slip with a name of a place. Give them two or three minutes to prepare a short sketch from the place. Everyone in the group should be involved.

4 Invite the groups to take turns and show their sketches to each other. Let the learners guess the places and the activities.

5 Prepare a simple story about places you visited with a magic wand. Let the learners listen and mime all the activities you do in the story. Pause during the story to give the learners enough time to mime. For example:

Yesterday when I woke up, I found a magic wand next to my bed. I waved it and said 'Abracadabra!'

Next I was on a beach and went for a swim in the sea.

Then I sat down on the sand and ate a fresh pineapple.

I waved the wand again. I was in the jungle. I walked through the jungle and it was not easy. I had to push all the big leaves to the side.

So I waved the magic wand and I rode an elephant instead. It was fun. I looked around and saw many green trees and colourful animals.

I waved the wand one more time. I was in the circus. I walked on the tightrope, and then juggled with five balls.

I waved the wand for the last time. I was back at home. I was so tired that I lay down on my bed.